Marc Antony Henderson

Songs of the Pacific. Or light on the Samoan question

Marc Antony Henderson

Songs of the Pacific. Or light on the Samoan question

ISBN/EAN: 9783744652049

Printed in Europe, USA, Canada, Australia, Japan

Cover: Foto ©Thomas Meinert / pixelio.de

More available books at **www.hansebooks.com**

SONGS

OF THE

PACIFIC.

OR

LIGHT ON THE SAMOAN QUESTION.

PACIFIC BANK, PUBLISHERS.

SAN FRANCISCO, CAL.

1889.

THESE rare gleanings of the South Sea Isles are here reproduced in the hope that the vivid picture they paint of the inner life and thoughts of these little-known races will be of great service in unraveling the troublesome Samoan question.

We feel sure that nothing has ever been offered to the American, German or British public of equal merit, bearing on this subject; and we certainly think that an intelligent perusal will convince the most sceptical that hydropathic treatment is the proper remedy for all those laboring under the hit-me-if-you-dare fever.

THE

Song of Milkanwatha

TRANSLATED FROM THE ORIGINAL SAMOAN-FEEJEE.

BY

MARC ANTONY HENDERSON, D. C. L.

PROFESSOR OF THE SAMOAN-FEEJEE AND SOUTH-SEA ISLANDS LANGUAGE
AND LITERATURE.

" There were who spiritual legends feigned,
Half lofty, half profound, not nigh half true."
Philip James Bailey.

" He, of a damsel, with fellow-maidens sporting,
In vital brilliance dropping through the star·gate
Of the high luminous land, was born;
And lifting into life his facial flower,
Throughout the vast passivity he passed,
All active; scaling on foot the mount,
That he his starry ancestry might hail,
There converse held, with all the eloquent orbs;
Adown a foamy torrent, in a skiff,
Dimpling the wave, he sped; great the show
Of lawny-weepers, lifted to dim eyes;
He fainted, asked the watery powers, and at last,
With eyne by spirit-fire purged, discerned
How sweet was truth, for death in truth was life.
Initiate, mystic, perfected, epopt,
Illuminate, adept, transcendent, he
Ivy-like lived, and died, and again lived,
Resuscitant—God of psycho-pompous function."

"*The Mystic.*"—PHILIP JAMES BAILEY.

TRANSLATOR'S PREFACE.

——:o:——

A WORD or two with reference to the following Poem which is herewith presented to the civilized world.

That, in many of its parts, there is a strong correspondence between it and Mr. Longfellow's great work, "The Song of Hiawatha," is too apparent to be overlooked. But so far from basing upon this similarity of incident and treatment, a charge of *literary piracy* against Mr. Longfellow, as has been done by some who have discovered a much fainter likeness to a poem of Scandinavian origin—the translator recognized in it only another evidence of that unity of thought which characterizes the human species. and which is a natural consequence of the unity of the races, of which the great family of man is composed.

How far the "Song of Hiawatha" may be justly deemed an *imitation*, however, in outline, incident, or versification, of the Scandinavian—or of the poem from the Feejee, here presented to our readers—it is for them and not the translator, to decide; but it is believed that a careful comparison, one with another, will disclose many curious resemblances in form and feature, which may be thought worthy the attention of men of letters.

It is hardly necessary to add that, so far as he was able to appreciate the spirit of the Poem, the translator has endeavored faithfully to retain it.

The liberties which he has taken have been verbal only, and such as are unavoidable in transplanting the ideas and emotions of a people from their own language to another.

For example, "Polli-wog-in" has been translated *farmers*, although the use of the word may seem a strange one to those into whose conception of the Feejee character the idea of *industry* has never entered.

The reason, however, is obvious—since our estimates of things are always *relative*, and he who keeps a pig or grows a square yard of potatoes among a people distinctively *savage*, judged by their standard of labor, is as emphatically a farmer, as the man who plows, in America, his hundred acres, and whose cattle graze upon a thousand hills.

Several words and forms of expression which in our language have become obsolete, such as her'n, his'n, ouch, not never, not for no one, didn't nothing, a-rolling, a-sitting, etc., are retained because of their striking analogy to words and expressions representing the same ideas in the Feejee tongue.

The word that designates the Water treatment which we call Hydropathy, is so rendered from the original, "Sit-an'-shiver."

If the objection be made to the scenes and characters as represented in the translation, that they indicate so advanced a stage of social progress as to suggest the probability of their having caught an unconscious coloring from the fancy of the translator, it may be fairly met with the presumption that a closer familiarity with the manners and mode of life of the Feejees, on the part of the reader, would show the invalidity of such objections.

To give an impulse to investigation in this direction is the translator's only motive in publication, and his earnest hope is that this simple Poem may serve to interest the Christian World in the people among whom it is still preserved, and in whose midst he has spent several memorable years.

ARGUMENT.

—:o:-—

THE Birth and Childhood of the Hero. His youth. He forms the acquaintance of two singular individuals. Goes courting and is married. His two friends swept away by the Watta-puddel, or Rushing River, to the land of Ponee-rag-bag, situr' farther downward. His wife is seized with chills . fever, and, being supposed dead, is thrown into tl river, but revived by the sudden shock of the wate is borne in safety to Ponee-rag-bag. The hero, in ι fit of temporary insanity, follows her in his skiff. Reaching Ponee-rag-bag, he finds not only his wife, but his friends also, awaiting him. Their strange preservation suggests the water treatment in disease, and returning with them he becomes the founder of the Hydropathic System.

The scene is laid in the Island of Chaw-a-man-up, one of the Feejee group.

THE SONG OF MILKANWATHA.

INTRODUCTION.

——:o:——

If an individual person,
Say John Smith,* or John Smith's uncle,
Or some other friend of his'n,
Should propound to me the question,
Whence derived you these traditions
Which you are about to tell us,
With their incidents peculiar;
These strange legends so mysterious,
With the smell of trees and flowers,
With the sound of brooks and breezes,
With the roaring of the thunder,
And the very wild beasts, also,
Ever sounding, never ceasing.
Going when you think it's stopping,
Going as a woman's tongue goes,
As a lively woman's tongue goes;
I would speak up, I would tell him,
" From the regions far beyond here,
From the mighty wildernesses

---

*The name John Smith, which occurs several times in the
following introduction, has been employed because, by conven-
tional use, it has come to express the idea of *man in the concrete.*

1*   **Pacific Bank Issues World Letters of Credit.**

Where the Ninkumpoops inhabit,
Where the Noodles pitch their wigwams,
From the hill-tops bare and breezy,
From the valleys soft and mushy,
From the marshes and the duck-ponds,
Where the melancholy bull-frog,
Brek-e-kex-co-ax, the bull-frog,
Sitteth in the slimy waters:
" As I heard them, so I tell them,
Literatim et verbatim,
Just exactly as I heard them
From the mouth of Rumpalumpkin,
Him as played upon the bagpipes,
Played—and sang between the blowings."
And if John Smith, or his uncle,
Or some other friend of his'n
Should inquire where Rumpalumpkin
Came across these strange traditions;
I would speak up, I would tell him,
" In the trees where climb the squirrels,
In the holes where crouch the woodchucks,
In the cracks the spiders hide in,
In the hornet's nests he found them;
" All—or nearly all—the wildfowl
Sang them, shrieked them, in the marshes,
In the marshes by the duck-ponds;
Pee-nee-wig the turkey-buzzard,
And the gray-goose Dab-si-dido;
Quag the duck, the snipe Lum-bago,
And the long-legged, bush-necked partridge,
Ringdam-bol le-meta-kimo."
And if John Smith, or his uncle,

Or some other friend of his'n,
Asked me, Who is Rumpalumpkin?
Tell us more of Rumpalumpkin;
I should speak up very quickly,
And reply to him in this way:
" In the valley of Mus-tug-gin,
That extremely verdant valley,
Where, in summer, green the trees were,
Bare and leafless in the winter;
Where the streams flowed in the Summer,
But in Winter time were frozen;
In this very verdant valley,
Lighted by the sparkling waters,
By the forest branches shaded,
Lived the man as played the bag-pipes,
Played— and sang between the blowings—
Lived the minstrel Rumpalumpkin."
Ye who like this sort of legend,
Like it well enough to listen,
Like the way the thing is done in,
Like a story so unmeaning,
That, to save your life, you cannot
See nor head nor tail un-*to* it,
Tell the end from the beginning—
Listen to this wondrous story,
To this Song of Milkanwatha.
Ye who will not writhe nor wriggle
While I tell this story to you,
Will not look and act uneasy,
But will give your whole attention,
Without gaping, stretching, yawning,
While I tell this story to you;

Listen now, for I will tell it,
Tell you truly, as I told you,
As I told you I would tell it,
On condition, you remember,
That you would not writhe nor wriggle,
But would give your whole attention
Without gaping, stretching, yawning;
While I tell this story to you;
Listen now all ye, I pray you,
Hear this Song of Milkanwatha.

I.

Milkanwatha's Childhood.

——:o:——

Long ago, in days that are not,
In the times that no one knows of,
Right head-foremost thro' the evening
From the shining planet Venus,
Swiftly down came Kimo-kairo,
Married, but without no children.
She was climbing up a plum-tree,
Plum-tree in the planet Venus,
Climbing with some other women,
When, alas, the branch she stood on
Cracked and snapped, because 'twas rotten,
Cracked and snapped off quite completely,
And head-foremost thro' the evening,
Fell the long-haired Kimo-kairò.
Fell the shrieking Kimo-kairo,
Fell the long-haired, shrieking Kimo,
Down to Plow-e-tup the cornfield,
In the cornfield soft and mushy.
" Look! a rocket!" said the farmers,
" Some one must have fired a rocket,
'Cause that was the stick that come down."
'Midst the chickweed and the clover,
Lying on some last year's huskings,
In the Plow-e-tup, the cornfield,
Kimo-kairo had a son born,
And she called him Milkanwatha,

Him as is our story's hero,
The real, genuine Milkanwatha.
But alas for Kimo-kairo!
And alas for Milkanwatha!
She, the mother, was so injured
Falling from the planet Venus,
Plum-tree in the planet Venus,
And the Plow-e-tup the cornfield
Was so very cool and open,
Such a breezy place to lie in,
That, to save her life, she could not,
Keep from dying while she lay there,
Lay upon the last year's huskings;
So she died, poor Kimo-kairo.
And beside her, Milkanwatha
Rolled and cried, unhappy baby,
Wond'ring why she didn't nurse him,
Thinking her alive as usual.

There they both were found next morning,
By the ancient nurse Marcosset;
Her whom all the neighbors honored
For her skill in nursing sick-folks,
Chiefly through the chills and fever:
There she found sweet Kimo-kairo
Lying dead upon the huskings;
And not far off—found our hero,
Very wide awake and kicking.

On the banks of Watta-puddel—
Rushing river, Watta-puddel—
Stood the ancient nurse's wigwam,
Stood the wigwam of Marcosset;
Back behind it dark the woods were,

Dark as pitch the woods behind it;
Swift before it rolled the river,
Rolled its torrent ever onward,
Through the long and dismal forests,
Through the mountains and the valleys,
In the sunlight and the moonlight,
Toward the unknown Ponee-rag-bag,
Toward the regions farther downward.
Here Marcosset, ancient female,
Nursed the baby Milkanwatha;
Gave him porridge, gave him catnip,
Gave him pap and water-gruel;
When he fretted, quickly hushed him,
Saying, "Bulldog, bite his toes off;"
Put him fast asleep by humming,
"Hitta-ka-dink, my duck, my darling,
Who's this with the funny snub-nose,
Snub-nose, so uncommon snubby?
Hitta-ka-dink, my duck, my darling."
Here he, day by day, grew older,
Sat alone upon the door-step,
Heard the summer breezes moaning,
Heard the waters ever plashing,
Sounds unusual and peculiar;
" Tizzarizzen," sighed the breezes—
" Splosh-ka-swosh-ky," plashed the river.
Here he saw the Melee-we-git,
Lightning-bug, the Melee-wee-git,,
Saw the Feesh-go-bang, mosquito,
Saw Snappo, the pinching-beetle,
Saw the dragon-fly, Snap-peter,
And the flea, too, Sticka-ta-wa-in.

Pacific Bank Sells Telegraphic Transfers.

Saw above him in the heavens,
The Aurora red and glowing—
Wondered what it was that did it—
Said, "What is that there, Marcosset?"
And Marcosset up and answered,
" Once an angry boy I know of,
Took and clutched his uncle To-bee,
Took and pitched him, in the evening,
Up into the starry heavens;
Right against the boulder pavement
Of the Milky-way he pitched him,
And his blood and brains went splashing
Over all the sky around there,
That's what makes them spots upon it—
That is why it's called Aurora."*
Saw the dazzling planet Venus,
Blushing o'er the dark horizon;
Said, "What-is that there, Marcosset?"
And Marcosset up and answered,
" That's the hole your mother fell through,
When she tumbled from the plum-tree—
Plum-tree in the planet Venus—
Down to Plow-e-tup the cornfield."
And whenever, in the evening,
Brek-e-kex-co-ax, the bull-frog,
Made all kinds of dismal noises,
Milkanwatba, trembling, whispered,
" What an awful noise; what does it?"
And Marcosset up and answered;

---

*A capital pun upon this word, in the original, is entirely lost in the translation.

" 'Tis the bull-frog's way of singing,
Singing to another bull-frog
In the marshes and the duck-ponds—
Only that, my Milkanwatha."
So, by slow degrees, it turned out,
That he learned the names of all things,
Of the birds, and beasts, and fishes,
Of the bugs of each description,
How they looked and where they hided,
And their general mode of living;
So he gained from old Marcosset,
Much important information,
Much which *we* can never know of
In our day and generation—
Our degenerate generation.

II.

Milkanwatha's Hunting.

——:o:——

Now, about this time, Sumpunkin,
He, the jolly wag, Sumpunkin,
He, the crony of Marcosset,
Made a very stylish blow-gun
For our hero, Milkanwatha;
Made it from a stalk of alder,
From a willow made some arrows,—
Little arrows for to blow through—
And each arrow had a pin in.
   This he gave to Milkanwatha,
For to keep, he said, remarking,
" You must go, my little fellow,
Go into the woods behind here,
Go and kill a pretty squirrel,
Go and kill a rather big one."
Right into the woods behind there
Ran the gallant Milkanwatha,
With his arrows and his blow-gun;
And he heard the birds exclaiming,
" Don't you blow at me your arrows,
Blow your arrows with a pin in,
Oh, now, Milkanwatha, don't you."
   Cried the O-pee-pod the bull-finch,
Cried the Nill-e-pip the chippy,
" Don't you blow at me your arrows,
With a pin in, Milkanwatha."

Pacific Bank Loans on Wheat.

On a stump, not far before him,
Hopped the Lingo-sneedel, smiling,
Hopped the Lingo-sneedel, blue-bird,
Sneezed, and cried out, after sneezing,
" Don't you blow at me your arrows,
With a pin in, Milkanwatha."
And a little off to one side,
Peeped the Yalla-gal, the wood-chuck,
Sort o' feared and sort o' not so,
Peeped and squeaked to Milkanwatha,
" Don't you blow at me your arrows
With a pin in, Milkanwatha."
Onward through the woods behind there,
Walked he, stalked he, with his blow-gun,
Heeding not these observations;
Neither O-pee-pod, the bull-finch,
Nor the Nill-e-pip, the chippy,
Nor the Yalla-gal, the wood-chuck,
Nor the blue-bird, Lingo sneedel—
He was hunting after squirrels,
After squirrels only, *he* was.
Crouching down behind an old log,
Pretty soon he saw a squirrel,
And it was a rather big one;
Saw a squirrel's head on one side—
Saw a squirrel's tail the other—
Head and tail of one big squirrel:
Taking in a long breath, very,
Milkanwatha aimed his blow-gun—
Blew through with the long breath, very,
With the long breath that he took in;
Squirrel's tail a moment quivered,

Squirrel closed his eyes a moment,
Turned a somerset, completely,
And lay dead upon the old log:
For the arrow, with the pin in,
To his brain had penetrated,
Like a big musquito, stung him,
    In the wilderness, behind there,
Far behind Marcosset's wigwam,
Far away from Watta-puddel,
Lay defunct Peek-week, the squirrel—
Lay without a breath or motion,
Hearing not the breeze's sighing,
Hearing not their Tizzarizzen,
As they moaned his sad condition,
As they sobbed, amid the branches,
O'er the death that he had come to,
O'er his speedy dissolution,
    But the victor, in his triumph,
Jumped and waived his hat, exulting
O'er the death that he had come to,
O'er his speedy dissolution;
And, with eager haste, he ran home,
In one hand Peek-week, the squirrel,
In the other hand the blow-gun—
Fearful instrument, the blow-gun;
And Marcosset and Sumpunkin, ·
Kissed him 'cause he killed the squirrel,
'Cause it was a rather big one.
From the squirrel-skin, Marcosset
Made some mittens for our hero,
Mittens with the fur-side, inside,
With the fur-side next his fingers

So's to keep the hand warm inside;
That was why she put the fur-side—
Why she put the fur-side, inside.
From the other parts, Marcosset—
From the lungs, and lights, and liver,
Brain, and heart, and spinal marrow—
Made a squirrel chowder for him;
And their friends dropped in to eat some;
Smacked their lips, while they were eating,
'Cause 'twas such a tender squirrel;
Smacked the lips of Milkanwatha,
After they had finished eating,
'Cause he was so bold a hunter;
Called him Good-boy, Mulee-donkee,
Called him Brave-boy, Spoo-ne-boo-bee.

III.

Milkanwatha's Youth and Early Manhood.

——:o:——

Milkanwatha, now, was older—
Older, bigger, than he had been
Since his mother, Kimo-kairo,
In the cornfield came and bore him.
None were half as big as he was,
None were half as tall as he was,
None were half as strong as he was;
None could lift the things that he could,
None could catch the things that he could,
None could eat the things that he could;
No one ever laughed so loudly,
As he laughed, when something funny,
Happened for to come across him;
Ever saw such sights as he did,
Ever thrashed so many rascals,
  He could take and fire an arrow—
Run right after—go right by it —
Then stop short and say, distinctly,
Always, "Jac," and sometimes, "Robbin-sun,"
Ere the lazy arrow got there.
  He could take and throw a stone so,
Throw it right up overhead so,
At the moment when the sun set,
That it wouldn't think of dropping,
Till the sun came up, next morning,
Till the Doodel-doo, the rooster,

Crowed the daylight up next morning.
He could do the Cutta-dido—
Cut the pigeon's wing so quickly,
That his heels would strike together,
Eighty times and even ninety—
Once he did it ninety-nine times—
One more would have made the hundred.
He had leggins, Roota-ba-ga,
That were quite peculiar leggins;
When they were put on and buttoned,
He could step from here to yonder,
Step from here, 'way over yonder,
Step right up on the horison,
And converse there, with the full moon.
He had Clog-a-logs, moreover,
Boots—with which, on one occasion,
While conversing with the full moon,
On the edge of the horison,
He, so fiercely, kicked his foot out,
That he hit the constellation,
Thimbel-nubbin, or Big Dipper—
Kicked a hole right in the bottom,
So that all the water ran through,
Which was put there, for the Great Bear,
For to come and wash his feet in.
All the eagles of the mountains
Flew far over Milkanwatha;
All the wild beasts of the forest
Trembled when he strided toward them,
Fled into the shadows trembling.
All the old men praised his courage,
All the young men owned him strongest;

All the women wished for children,
Wished for sons as brave as he was;
All the maidens gazed upon him,
Gazed with silent admiration,
Gazed with beating hearts and blushes,
As he passed their lonely wigwams,
And returned with sighs and weeping,
To their usual avocations;
Wishing, as they darned their stockings—
Scrubbed, and baked, and swept, and dusted,
Did clear-starching, did crochet-ing,
Made pin-cushions, always heart-shaped,
Fastened, two and two, together,
Pierced all o'er with pins like arrows,
Arrows from an unseen archer—
Wishing that a gallant lover,
That a lover, like our hero,
Soon might come, and sit beside them
In their wigwams; each one wishing
He was her'n, and she was his'n,
Ever her'n, and ever his'n,
Her'n and his'n, now and ever;
Each one wishing for our hero—
But he wishing not for no one;
Having other things to think of,
Other fish upon his griddle,
Other fish to fry upon it.

IV.

Milkanwatha's Friends.

— —:o:— —

Friends enough, had Milkanwatha;
Some he liked and some he didn't,
Some were true, and some were false ones;
But a couple of the former,
He was very special fond of;
Silli-ninkum, the sweet piper,
And the very fat man, Bee-del.
Milkanwatha's oldest crony
Was the piper, Silli-ninkum,
Him as was the best of pipers,
Him as piped, as no one else piped;
Soon as he began a piping,
Came the people for to hear him;
Came the young men, and the old men,
Came the matrons, and the maidens,
Came the nurses, and the children,
For to hear him do his piping;
Sometimes he would set 'em laughing—-
Set 'em all a crying sometimes,
'Cording as the tune was jolly,
Or forlorn and melancholy.
He would play so very softly,
That the breezes stopped to hear him,
That the squirrels ceased to chatter,
That the Yalla-gal, the woodchuck
In his rapture, curled his tail up,

And the bluebird, Lingo-sneedel,
Stood on one leg for to listen.
Silli-ninkum, the sweet piper,
Was beloved by Milkanwatha.
'Cause he piped as no one else piped,
'Cause he always was obliging—
Piping when requested for to.
But, beside him, Milkanwatha
Loved the very fat man, Bee-del;
He, the fattest human being,
That you ever laid your eyes on.
From his very earliest childhood,
He was round, and fat, and lazy;
Didn't go a-squirrel hunting,
Didn't skate and didn't nothing—
Wasn't like the other children;
But they understood the reason,
And they all were sorry for him,
'Cause he was of such a fatness—
'Cause his fatness grew upon him.
Once his mother said un-*to* him,
" Bee-del, you are good for nothing;
Always hanging 'round the wigwam,
Waddling round about the village,
Lying, sprawled out, in the sunshine;
You had best be doing something."
Not a word did Bee-del answer,
Not an observation made he,
But he waddled from the corner,
From the wigwam slowly waddled,
Went and stood upon the hillside,
Slowly sat down, slowly laid down,

Doubled up and started rolling,
Rolled right onward, forward, downward,
Down the green and sloping hillside,
Down the hillside kept a-rolling;
And his mother stood and watched him,
Wond'ring when he'd stop a-rolling.

Nothing more was heard of Bee-del,
For six months and something over;
But, one morning, while a-baking,
Bee-del's mother heard a rumbling,
Like a big stone, tumbling downward
From the hill-top, up before her;
Went and looked, and there came Bee-del,
Came the fat man, rolling, rumbling,
Came a-rolling toward the wigwam,
Came and rolled in through the back door,
Rolled right up into the corner,
And remained rolled up, in silence.

He had been, for six months, rolling,
Six months and a little over;
Rolling on from morn to evening,
And from season unto season,
Through all countries, nations, climates,
Past the zones and past the tropics,
Past the line of the equator,
Ever onward, forward, downward,
Till he got to where he came from—
Till he all the earth had rolled round.

These two persons just referred to,
Silli-ninkum, the sweet piper,
And the very fat man, Bee-del,
As I've mentioned, were the couple—

Were the friends of Milkanwatha—
Whom he liked uncommon strongly;
And these three, this faithful trio,
Never quarreled with each other,
Never gossiped, never back-bit,
Never acted mean, as some do,
But they did as they'd be done by,
And they often met together,
And indulged in conversation
In a free and easy manner.

V.

Milkanwatha's Courtship and Marriage.

——:o:——

Just as, to a big umbrella,
Is the handle, when it's raining,
So a wife is, to her husband;
Though the handle do support it,
'Tis the top keeps all the rain off;
Though the top gets all the wetting,
'Tis the handle bears the burden;
So the top is good for nothing,
If there isn't any handle,
And the case holds, vice versa.
In this way, did Milkanwatha
Reason, when he was a-thinking,
Thinking of his Pogee-wogee,
Of the blue-eyed Sweet-Potato,
In the village of the Noodles.
" Marry some one living round here,"
Said the ancient nurse, Marcosset;
" Don't go looking over yonder,
For to find a wife to marry;
As a stick of maple candy,
Is the homliest girl around here;
As a lozenge or a gum-drop
Is the prettiest over yonder."
And thus answered Milkanwatha:
" Very true, dear old Marcosset,
Mighty sweet is maple candy,

Pacific Bank Loans on Wheat.

But I much prefer a lozenge—
Very much prefer a gum-drop."
    Said Marcosset, "Don't you go, now,
For to get a girl to marry,
Knowing nothing whatsoever;
Bring one as can do clear-starching,
Sew, and knit, and run of errands,
And be generally useful—
That's the sort of girl to marry."
    Milkanwatha answered, cheerful;
" In the regions far beyond here,
Where the Noodles pitch their wigwams,
Pogee-wogee, Sweet-Potato,
Charming female, is residing;
I will go, and fetch her to you,
And she'll make herself convenient,
Sew, and knit, and do clear-starching,
Be your lozenge, be your gum-drop,
Be your stick of maple candy "
    " Don't you go now," said Marcosset,
" Go and fetch an unknown female,
Don't you go and fetch a Noodle—
Awful strange folks, are the Noodles."
    Then replied our Milkanwatha;
That's exactly why I do it,
'Cause they're strange, and mustn't be so;
We must make ourselves acquainted,
We must go and call upon them."
Saying which, our hero, boldly,
Traveled to the regions northward,
Past the dreary wildernesses,
Where the Ninkumpoops inhabit,

To the village of the Noodles.
He had put on Roota-ba-ga,
Buttoned on the magic leggins,
And, although he kept a-stepping,
From one hill-top to another,
Over ·cornfields, soft and mushy,
Over marshes, goose-ponds, duck-ponds,
Yet he seemed a long while, getting
To the home of Pogee-wogee,
To the village of the Noodles.
Shortly previous to arriving,
He perceived a woodchuck, peeping—
Peeping from his hole, for fresh air,
Cause 'twas badly ventilated,
But the woodchuck didn't see him;
So he took and kicked his foot out,
And he knocked the woodchuck's brains out—
Just as when he hit the bottom
Of the Dipper, Thimbel-Nubbin,
All the water went and ran through,
Which was put there, for the Great Bear,
For to come and wash his feet in.
Then he took the woodchuck with him,
For a gift to Pogee-wogee;
" Who is that?" inquired a Noodle—
" That's the hero Milkanwatha;"
" What's he got?" "He's got a woodchuck."
Pogee-wogee's loving grandma
At the front door sat, a-knitting,
And, beside her, Sweet Potato,
Charming female, was a-sitting,
Looking somewhat melancholy.

The old lady's mind was busy—
Busy as her trembling fingers;
Far away her thoughts were flitting,
Midst the days so long departed,
Midst the memories of girlhood,
Midst the sunny moments flitting;
Flitting midst them, as, so often,
With the dear ones gone forever,
She had seen, in youthful rambles
Bees, on restless wing pass lightly
Lightly on from flower to flower,
Humming low, melodious music,
Sporting, gayly, in the sun-shine.
Pogee's thoughts were busy also,
Busy as her grandma's fingers;
She was thinking of our hero,
Wond'ring why she'd never met him,
Never heard his well-known footstep,
Never seen his sturdy figure,
Since that time when they had parted,
Since that sunny summer morning.
In the midst of these reflections,
Midst the thoughts that passed before them,
Unexpected, round a corner,
Rather wet with perspiration,
Holding in his hand the woodchuck,
Came the lover—ardent lover
Of the Noodle, Pogee-wogee,
Came the son of Kimo-kairo,
Came the joyous Milkanwatha.
Ancient grandame stopped her knitting,
Laid the stocking in the window,

Asked him to come in, remarking,
" Glad to see you, Milkanwatha."
    In the lap of Pogee-wogee
Milkanwatha laid the woodchuck,
And she looked at him so tender,
That his blood ran cold within him,
Saying, with a bashful softness,
" Very happy for to see you—
Very much so, Milkanwatha."
    Soon as he was seated, almost,
Pogee-wogee fetched refreshments,
Cause he looked so hot and tired,
Cause he had such perspiration;
Fetched him in some "floating island,"
Interspersed with pickled walnuts,
Which he much preferred of all things;
And a little mug of cider,
For to take and wash it down with,
Wash the floating isle and walnuts,
Isle and pickled walnuts down with.
    Not a word spoke Pogee-wogee,
But she heard the conversation
Going on, while he was feeding,
Heard him tell of old Marcosset—
How she found him, how she nursed him,
Gave him porridge, gave him catnip,
Gave him pap and water gruel;
Heard him tell of Silli-ninkum,
And the very fat man, Bee-del,
How the former piped uncommon,
And the latter rolled the earth round;
Heard him give a fine description,

Of the scenery about there,
On the banks of Watta-puddel.
" You have never been to see us,
  On the banks of Watta-puddel—
You nor any other Noodles;
Shall we never scrape acquaintance ?"
Said the ardent Milkanwatha.
    " That this may be obviated,
State of things be put a stop to,
S'pose you give me Pogee-wogee,
For to be a wife un-*to* me—
Sweet-Potato, charming female,
Much the handsomest of Noodles "—
    For some minutes, the old lady
Smoked her solemn pipe in silence;
Putting on her glasses, slowly,
First she looked at Pogee-wogee,
Then she looked at Milkanwatha;
" It depends on Pogee-wogee—
That's your feeling on the subject;
Speak your mind and heart out, Pogee."
    And the charming Sweet-Potato,
To the very ear-tips blushing,
With a dubious expression,
Crossed the wigwam to her lover,
Drew her stool up, saying faintly,
" You may have me if you want to—
I'll go with you, Milkanwatha."
    Such was Milkanwatha's courting,
This was just the way he did it,
Bore his darling, Pogee-wogee,
From her grandma's lonely cabin,

From the village of the Noodles;
Back he bore her thro' the forests,
Over hills, and over valleys,
To the ancient nurse's wigwam—
To the wigwam of Marcosset.
All along the line of travel,
Birds were singing to the lovers,
Songs of welcome 'mid the branches,
Songs of warm congratulation,
And the bugs joined in the chorus;
Sang the Opee-pod, the bullfinch,
Sang the Nillee-pip, the chippy,
Sang the blue-bird, Singo-sneedel;
Hummed the Feesh-go-bang, musquito,
Hummed Snappo, the pinching-beetle,
And the dragon-fly, Snap-peter;
" Aint it lucky, aint it lucky,
Jolly luck for Pogee wogee,
Jolly luck for Milkanwatha."
So he fetched her to Marcosset,
Fetched the lozenge, fetched the gum-drop
Fetched the stick of maple candy,
Pogee-wogee, Sweet-Potato,
Loveliest of female Noodles.
They arrived on Tuesday morning,
And were married Thursday evening;
All day Tuesday, old Marcosset,
Made her pies and preparations;
All day Wednesday, boys were running
Up and down, throughout the village,
For to leave a soda-cracker,
At the door of every wigwam,

As a card of invitation—
As a sign that Milkanwatha
Meditated matrimony.

   Thursday came, and Thursday evening,
And the neighbors, also, with it;
Fast they crowded in the wigwam,
Crowded in the pies and puddings,
Which Marcosset made, on Tuesday;
But the bride, nor bridegroom neither,
Didn't eat a bit of nothing,
Only waited on the others,
Only watched the pies and puddings
Disappearing, in succession,
In the stomachs of the people.

   When the eating part was over,
There was singing, piping, dancing,
And the evening went so swiftly
That it left the guests behind it;
Left them 'mid the hours of morning.

   Then they called for Silli-ninkum,
For to sing a song at parting;
And he came the skillful Piper,
Him as always was obliging,
Piping when requested for to—
Came and sang the song that follows,
Sang the verses twixt the blowings,
Sang a female's lamentation
For her lover, her Bee-no-nee:

  " When I think of him I love so,
Oh, lor! think of him I love so,
When I am a-thinking of him—
Ouch! my sweetheart, my Bee-no-nee!

" Oh, lor! when we left each other,
He presented me a thimble,
As a pledge, a silver thimble—
Ouch! my sweetheart, my Bee-no-nee!

" 'I'il go 'long with you,' he whispered,
'Oh, lor! to the place you came from,
Let me go along,' he whispered—
Ouch! my sweetheart, my Bee-no-nee!

" 'It's awful fur, full fur,' I answered,
'Fur away it is, I answered,
Oh, lor, yes! the place I came from'—
Ouch! my sweetheart, my Bee-no-nee!

" As I looked round for to see him
Where I left him, for to see him,
He was looking for to see me—
Ouch! my sweetheart, my Bee-no-nee!

" On the log he was a-sitting.
On the hollow log a-sitting,
That was chopped down by somebody—
Ouch! my sweetheart, my Bee-no-nee!

" When I think of him I love so,
Oh, lor! think of him I love so,
When I am a-thinking of him—
Ouch! my sweetheart, my Bee-no-nee!"

When this mornful song was ended
All the folks seemed in a hurry
For to go, and so they did it,
Leaving there the nurse Marcosset,
With the bride and with the bridegroom;
And they all three started eating,
And continued so till morning—
Till the doodle-doo, the rooster,
Crowed the daylight up next morning.

VI.

Pa-Pa-Mama.

——:o:——

You shall hear how Pa-pa-mama,
Pogee-wogee's whilome lover,
* In the village of the Noodles,
Came one time to Watta-puddel;
How he showed himself a coward,
How he proved himself a rascal,
How he reached his dissolution.

It was in the sprinkly Spring-time,
That he came to Watta-puddel;
Came with bitter thoughts inside him,
Came to be revenged on Pogee,
'Cause she had in times departed,
When he asked her to be his'n,
Strongly urged her to be his'n—
Said with pitying glance, but firmly,
  " Never your'n, O Pa-pa-mama!
No," she muttered, " never his'n."

Through the village, sneaking came he,
At the dusky hour of twilight,
When the people all were gathered,
As their custom was to do so,
Met together, story telling,
In the fat man, Bee-del's wigwam;
Just as Bee-del was describing
What he witnessed while a-rumbling,
All the earth around, a-rumbling

On his swift, mysterious journey,
And the people listened to him,
Winking when he wasn't looking,
Much as if to say, " We know him,
Know him we do, you and me do."
  He had seen, he said, a river
Bigger than the Watta-puddel,
And so muddy too, said Bee-del,
That a spoon stands straight up in it!
And the people pointed slowly
Over the left shoulder, saying,
" Oh now, Bee-del, what a story,
Boo!" they said, " you're telling, Bee-del."
  On this river deep and muddy,
Swam a monster like a sturgeon,
Fatter than ten thousand sturgeons,
And his fins, instead of flapping,
Round and round continued turning,
Quite as fast as I myself did.
" Boo!" the people cried together,
" Boo!" they said, "it's such a big one."
  On his head, he said, were growing,
Straight and tall as is the pine-tree,
Two black tusks all hollow inside;
And his breath, so dark and dismal,
Dark as thunder clouds in summer,
Through them rolled forth o'er the river
Darkening all the landscape over.
" Boo!" they said, " it's Bee-del talking"
  Round his mouth, like summer lightning,
Flames of fire flashed in the darkness,
And the monster, while a-swimming,

Shrieked so wildly, that the echoes
On the far-off misty hill-sides,
On the hill-sides far below there,
Up and answered to his shrieking,
Answered as the tigress answers
To the tiger in the forest.
" Boo! " they said, "a likely story! "
  On his back were huddled, shrinking,
Men and women, pale and shrinking,
Pale faced as the moon in winter;
Borne off by the fiery monster—
For the prey of him and his'n,
Borne off, as the tiger swiftly
Bears his victim through the darkness,
Bears it to his forest hiding.
And the people winking, whispered,
" What a liar is our Bee-del!
Boo! " they said "what lies he tells us."
  In the meantime, Pa-pa-mama
Stealing through the silent evening
Reached the wigwam of Marcosset;
" No one here," he said rejoicing,
" Coast all clear," he said, exulting;
" All the folks have gone to Bee-del's."
  With a mushy step he entered,
Turned the tables bottom upside,
Turned the chairs all upside downside,
Kicked the boiling kettle over,
Piled the bed clothes in the corner,
Crammed the bolster up the chimney,
For to trouble Pogee-wogee,
For to make Marcosset angry;

After which he started homeward,
On his stealthy journey started.
  When our hero, shortly after,
Came and saw the wild disorder,
" Not so long," said he, " his legs are,
But I'll catch this fellow quickly."
  'Bout a mile or so he'd traveled,
On the track of Pa-pa-mama,
When he saw, just on before him,
Pa-pa-mama disappearing,
Slowly sinking in a mudhole,
Saw his head just going under;
And he stepped up very briskly,
Shouting down into the mud-hole,
" Never more, O Pa-pa-mama!
Will you drop into our wigwam;
You have dropped in once too often;
Turned the tables are forever—
You have done your final dropping;"
Then the hole closed up forever.
  But the people of the village
Still remembered Pa-pa-mama;
And whenever in the winter,
While they're sitting story-telling,
Comes the storm-wind from the Northland,
Rattling all the doors and windows,
Drifting snow around the wigwam;
" Lo! " they say, " 'tis Pa-pa-mama,
Turning all things wrong side upside,
Turning all things upside downside—
" 'Tis that Pa-pa-mama's doings."

VII.

The Fever and the Ague.

——:o:——

Fifteen summers, fifteen winters,
Fifteen springs, and fourteen autumns,
Full of joys and full of sorrows,
Now had passed since Milkanwatha,
Bore the beauteous Pogee-wogee
To the banks of the Watta-puddel;
Full of joys, with wife and children,
Full of griefs, for friends departed.
  Silli-ninkum, the sweet piper,
Him as piped as no one else piped,
He had passed to Ponee-rag-bag,
To the regions down the river;
He had done his final piping
On the banks of Watta-puddel.
  Going out, one winter morning,
For a little private skating,
Lo! the ice gave way beneath him!
Lo! the chilling waters seized him!
Bore him, struggling, ever downward,
To the country far below there,
To the regions down the river!
  Bee-del, too, was there no longer,
Milkanwatha's friend, the fat man;
He had left the field of action,
Left the banks of Watta-puddel.
  Since the piper had departed

He had grown a great deal fatter,
In his grief for having lost him,
Grown so fat he seldom waddled
Through the village as aforetime,
Only hung around the wigwam,
Sprawled himself out in the sunshine:
But one day, in fiery August,
After quite a hearty dinner,
He went down, he rolled himself down,
To the river for to bathe there,
As in days so long departed,
When he washed himself more often;
Far into the stream he waded,
And, alas! the current seized him!
As it seized poor Silli-ninkum;
In its wild embrace it clasped him,
And by reason of his fatness,
Of his stomach's monstrous fatness,
Which prevented him from striking,
Striking out his legs as usual—
He was carried, like a bladder,
Floating on the turbid waters,
To the land of Ponce-rag-bag,
To the regions farther downward.
　Never jumps a sheep that's frightened.
Over any fence whatever,
Over wall, or fence, or timber,
But a second follows after,
And a third, upon the second,
And a fourth, and fifth, and so on,
First a sheep and then a dozen,
Till they all, in quick succession,

One by one have got clean over:
So misfortunes, almost always,
Follow after one another,
Seem to watch each other, always,
When they see the tail uplifted,
In the air the tail uplifted,
As the sorrow leapeth over;
Lo! they follow, thicker, faster,
Till the air of earth seems darkened,
With the tails of sad misfortunes,
Till our hearts, within us, weary,
Cry out: "Are there more a-coming?"
So, alas, our Milkanwatha,
Ten years after he was married,
In that most uncommon winter,
Cried out: "Are there more a-coming?"
.   O that most uncommon winter!
O that sneezy, freezy winter!
Ever faster! faster!! faster!!!
Fell the snow, on vale and hill-side;
Ever colder! colder!! colder!!!
Swept the wild winds from the Northland,
Swept the storm-wind Gus-ta-blo-za!
It was really inconvenient,
Merely to step out a moment,
And, to go to any distance,
'Less you muffled up, completely,
In your tippet and your mittens,
Wasn't possible, by no means,
Without getting badly frost-bit.
    O! the Fever and the Ague!
O! the burning of the Fever!

O! the shaking of the Ague!
O! the way the children took it!
O! the way the mothers, also,
Took the Fever and the Ague!!
 To the ancient nurse's wigwam,
Came the two unpleasant strangers,
Came without an invitation,
Sat them down by Pogee, boldly,
Staring at the female Noodle!
One of them spoke up, remarking,
" I am Fever, Doan-chu-no-me! "
And the other one continued,
" I am Ague, Wot-el-sha-ku!! "
 But the frightened Pogee, shrinking,
Kept a-shaking and a-burning,
'Cause the Fever and the Ague,
Came and sat so close beside her,
'Cause they stared so steady at her.
 Right into the woods behind there,
Swiftly, madly, Milkanwatha
Rushed, to go and find the doctors—
All the doctors round about there,
And the ancient nurse Marcosset,
She so skilled in chills and fever,
Gave her warm drinks for to cure her,
For to try and take the chill off.
 Then the doctors, Nau-she-atus,
Six in all, came in to see her;
Two and two they came together,
Came and marched three times around her;
Then went up *one* to the bed-side:
" Put your tongue out, Pogee-wogee;"

" Hi-ai-ai!" said all the doctors;
Ho-ang-ho! the queer old doctors.
And another, went observing,
Pogee-Wogee's got the Ague;
Hi-ai-ai! said all the doctors,
Ho-ang-ho! the queer old doctors.
And a third one followed, saying,
Pretty soon she'll have the Fever;
Hi-ai-ai! said all the doctors—
Ho-ang-ho! the queer old doctors.
Then the other three did likewise;
After which they marched together,
Two and two around the bedstead,
Marched out from Marcosset's wigwam,
In the manner they had entered;
Hi-ai-ai! the wise old doctors—
Ho-ang-ho! the wondrous doctors.
    But, alas, for Pogee-wogee!
And, alas, for Milkanwatha!
She, the loveliest of Noodles
Was so scorched up by the Fever,
So much shook up by the Ague,
That she spoke nor moved no longer,
And our hero, disappointed,
Wrap her in a heavy blanket,
In the very neatest manner,
'Cording to the village custom;
And they bore her to the river,
In a long and sad procession;
And they stood and dropped her in it,
As their custom was to do so;
And the eager waters clasped her,

Bore her body as it had done,
In the case of him, the piper,
In the case of him, the fat man,
To the land of Ponee-rag-bag,
To the regions farther downward.
" Float on down," said Milkanwatha,
" Float on down, my duck, my darling,
Very soon, I'll follow after,
To the regions down the river,
I shall be along, my darling,
Be along, my duck, directly,
Be along, my duck, my darling—
Float on, float, and keep a-floating."

VIII.

Milkanwatha's Departure to Ponee-rag-bag.

——:o:——

Going now among the people,
On the banks there, standing, gazing,
" Lo!" he told them, "I am going,
I am going, now, to leave you,
Going down the Watta-puddel,
To the region of the sunset,
To the hole the sun drops into,
Over yonder red horizon—
Where you've, often, seen me standing,
And conversing with the full-moon—
And I shan't be back, at present,
Not for quite a lengthy season;
Take care of yourselves, my people,
Take much care," said Milkanwatha.
  Then he quickly pushed his skiff off,
Got aboard and floated in it,
Down the river's rushing current,
In the sunlight, and the moonlight,
Floating towards the Western sunset—
On his silent journey floated,
And the people standing, gazing,
Saw him bobbing, bobbing, bobbing,
Up and down upon the river,
Saw his Lawni-weeper waiving,
Saw his handkerchief a-waiving,
Far adown the Watta-puddel;

And they all continued calling,
" Good-bye, good-bye, Milkanwatha;"
And the gray goose, Dab-si-di-do,
O'er the troubled waters flying,
Screamed out, " Good-bye, Milkanwatha,"
And the Yalla-gal, the woodchuck,
Squeaked out " Good-bye, Milkanwatha;"
And the melancholy bull frog,
Brek-e-kex-co-ax, the bull-frog,
On the river's slimy margin,
Echoed, " Good-bye," Milkanwatha.
  So it was that Milkanwatha,
Him as is our story's hero,
Floated down the Rushing river,
Floated thro' the fields and forests,
Thro' the vales and mountains floated,
Ever bobbing, bobbing, bobbing,
In the moonlight and the sunlight,
To the country of the sunset,
To the regions farther downward,
To the land of Ponee-rag-bag,
Far adown the rushing river—
Rushing river, Watta-puddel.

CONCLUSION.

——:o:——

When the hero of our legend
Reached the land of Ponee-rag-bag,
Reached the hole the sun drops into,
Lo! an unexpected pleasure
Waited for him, on the landing;
In her blanket wet and dripping,
Just as much alive as usual,
Stood there, smiling, on the landing,
Pogee—loveliest of Noodles.
For the water's sudden coldness,
From her silent stupor waked her,
From the swooning of the Fever,
Which, in vain, the wise old doctors,
Which the Ague, vainly shaking,
Tried to make her wake up out of,
In the wigwam of Marcosset;
And our hero, rushing to her,
Clasped her in his arms exclaiming,
" Lo! I see my duck, my darling,
See the moral of this matter,
See the lesson that it teaches;
What the Allopathic Practice
Was unable to accomplish,
Lo! how quickly was effected
By the Plunge-bathe, and the Blanket,
By the use of *Hydropathy.*
We must go back, Pogee darling,
Oh lor! to the place we come from,

We must hasten to our people,
And disclose to them this system,
Glorious system—Hydropathy."
    And they found there Silli-ninkum,
And the fat man, Bee-del, also,
In the same mysterious manner
Rescued from the hand of Danger—
From the jaws of Dissolution;
And they all went back together,
And he told the grateful people
How to drive off all diseases,
By the Plunge-bath and the Blanket—
By the use of Hydropathy.
    To this day they are residing,
Free from fear of chills and fever—
" Worst of ills that flesh is heir to,"
Darkest shadow o'er our pathway,
From the present to the future,
From the ' is now ' to the ' shall be '
To this hour, they are residing
In their village, by the river;
And our hero *doubly* liveth—
On the banks of Watta-puddel—
In the hearts of all his people,
When he taught the Bath and Blanket—
Glorious system—Hydropathy.

Pacific Bank is a Quarter of a Century Old.

NOTES.

PAGE 10.   *Brek-e-kex-co-ax, the bull-frog.*

The scholar will be reminded of the "Frogs" of Aristophanes. The word is one of a vast number which might be referred to in evidence of the fact that "Feejee" and "Greek," are derived from a common root--and the translator has no hesitation in asserting his conviction, that the early inhabitants of Greece—the Pelasgians—were colonists from these islands. The question is much too large for discussion here.

PAGE 10.   *Literatim et verbatim.*

The introduction of this familiar Latinism will not, it is hoped, be deemed in bad taste, when it is remembered that our own language furnished no proper substitute. In the original it reads, "Li-ka-zah-lee, Jus-sa-zak-lee."

PAGE 13.   *Kimo-kairo, or Pretty Pollie,*

Is a favorite name with the Feejese. It is probably taken from the fable of the "Parrot and the Partridge," a verse of which is quoted below—dropping, of course, the Feejee characters, but retaining, as nearly as possible, the sound of the original.

> " Kimo-kairo, delto, mairo,
> Kimo-kairo, kimo?
> Strim-stram pom a diddel,
> Lath-a-bon-ne, rig-dam—
> Rig-dam-bol-le-meta-kimo!"

PAGE 22.   *Always "Jac" and sometimes "Robbin-sun."* •

The reader will perceive that to this language we are indebted for the expression: " Before you can say Jack Robinson."

PAGE 24. *Did clear-starching, did crochet-ing.*

It is believed that these terms more clearly define to the English mind, the nature of the operations alluded to, than any others. Goats' milk, however, is used instead of starch—and its effect is to soften rather than to stiffen the material. All work of the latter sort—knitting, netting, etc., is done upon the thumbs, without the aid of needles, in a manner which cannot be described.

PAGE 29. *Just as to a big umbrella.*

Umbrellas are known to have been in use in these islands, from the earliest times. They are, invariably, constructed of sheet tin.

PAGE 34. *Pulling on her glasses, slowly.*

The Feejee women, of all ages, are proverbially near-sighted. In the other islands of the Pacific, the phrase, "as blind as a Feejee," is often heard. The date of the invention of spectacles is unknown.

PAGE 34. *To the very earlips blushing.*

This expression is remarkable—not because of its poetic merit only—but from the fact that it has been adopted by two poets of our own. In Keats' Endymion, we find, "those ears,
"Whose tips are glowing hot,"
and in the "Life Drama," by the "modern Shakspeare," as Alexander Smith has been aptly designated by several of the prominent English reviews, occurs the line,
"Hot to the ear-tips, with great thumps of heart."

PAGE 51. *Worst of ills that flesh is heir to.*

The striking parellelism between this line and the oft-quoted passage from Hamlet's Soliloquy:
"The thousand natural shocks that flesh is heir to,"
may excite some surprise. In the poem it will be seen that it appears as a quotation—not from the English bard as some might suppose —but from Tremen-jus, a Feejee poet who flour-

---

ished about the year thirteen. We give the passage in which it occurs, put into the mouth of a war-chief, while vainly endeavoring to devour an old enemy, captured in battle.

> " Thou tough soul! eating of whom be toil!
> Juiceless, thin, of bone compact, and sinew,
> Whereto pertaineth flavor, deathful strong;
> Not for food adapt, save of swiny heard,
> Boar-marshalled, tiger thunder-begotten,
> Or solar wolf! Famished were I,
> Youthfuller, such as not, then less heeded;
> Thus being, cannot I meat introduct
> Of mould o'er-tasteful, all pervasive, rank,
> Of ills flesh be th' heir to, worst much, may be !"

It must be borne in mind, however, that the poem in question was written in ruder times.

At the period of the translator's residence in Chaw-a-man-up, the practice of cannibalism had been, for many years, abandoned, and in other islands of the group, the minds of the people were so far enlightened that human flesh was indulged in only on Sundays.

PAGE 51. *Whom he taught the Bath and Blanket.*

The period of the introduction of the water treatment into this island cannot be definitely fixed, but it is supposed to vary little from the date of the downfall of the Roman Empire.

Milkanwatha, the hero of the Legend and the founder of the System, now ranks among the highest of the Feejee divinities. His name is held religiously sacred, and he is always addressed as the "god of the psycho-pompous function."

Much additional information concerning him may be found in the translator's forthcoming work, "The Cyclopædia of Feejee Literature,"

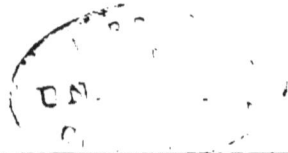

VOCABULARY.

Brek-e-kex-co-ax.................................Bull-frog.
Bee-del..Fat man.
Bee-no-nee ... .Dear darling.
Boo... ... .Pshaw!
Clog-a-logs......................................Boots.
Cutta-dido..................................Pigeon's wing.
Doan-chu-no-me...............................Fever.
Doodel-doo......................................Rooster.
Feesh-go-bang..................................Musquito.
Gusta-blo-za............................Storm-wind.
Hi-ai-ai..................................Yes, of course.
Hitta-ka dink..............................Lullaby.
Ho-ang-ho.................................Yes, by all means.
Kimo-kairo.................................Pretty Pollie.
Lawni-weeper..............................Handkerchief.
Lingo-sneedel.................................Bluebird.
Lum-ba-go...................................Snipe.
Marcosset..................................Ancient Nurse.
Me-le-wee-get ....Lightening-bug.
Milkanwatha.....................................Star-born.
Mulee-donkee............................Good boy.
Mus-tug-gin.............................Verdant valley.
Ninkumpoops................................ Feejee tribe.
Nil-le-pip.................................Chippie.
Noodles...................................Feejee tribe.
Nau-she-a-tus ....Doctors.
O-pee-pod ....Bullfinch.
Pa-pa-mama.............................Storm-fool.
Peek-week.................................Squirrel.
Pee-ne-wig................................Turkey buzzard.
Plow-et-tup...............................Corn-field.
Pogee-wo-gee ....Sweet-potato.

Po-nee-rag-bag.............................Land far down.
Quag...Duck.
Rig-dam-bol-le-met-a-kimo.................Partridge.
Roo-ta-ba-ga...............................Magic leggins.
Rum-pa-lump-kin............................Sweet singer.
Snap-po...................................Pinching-beetle.
Snap-peter.................................Dragon-fly.
Silli-ninkum..............................Sweet piper.
Splosh-ka-swosh-ky.........................Sound of water.
Sticka-ta-wa-in............................Flea.
Shoo-ne-boo-be............................Brave boy.
Sum-punk-in...............................Jolly wag.
Wot-el-sha-ku.............................Ague.
Thimbel-nubbin............................Big Dipper.
Tiz-za-riz-zen............................Sound of breezes.
Watta-puddel..............................Rushing river.
Yal-la-gal................................Woodchuck.